World Issues

CAPITAL PUNISHMENT

Alex Woolf

Chrysalis Children's Books

WORLD ISSUES

ABORTION	EQUAL OPPORTUNITIES	HUMAN RIGHTS
ANIMAL RIGHTS	EUTHANASIA	POVERTY
ARMS TRADE	FOOD TECHNOLOGY	RACISM
CAPITAL PUNISHMENT	GENETIC ENGINEERING	REFUGEES
CONSUMERISM	GENOCIDE	TERRORISM
DRUGS		

First published in the UK in 2004 by
(6) Chrysalis Children's Books
An imprint of Chrysalis Books Group plc
The Chrysalis Building, Bramley Road, London W10 6SP

Produced by Tall Tree Ltd

Editorial Manager: Joyce Bentley
Editor: Clare Lewis
Project Editor: Jon Richards
Designer: Ben Ruocco
Picture Researcher: Lorna Ainger
Educational Consultant: Lizzy Bacon

ISBN: 1 84458 080 6

British Library Cataloguing in Publication Data for this book is available from the British Library.

Printed in Hong Kong

10 9 8 7 6 5 4 3 2 1

Picture Acknowledgments
The Publishers would like to thank the following for their kind permission to reproduce the photographs:
AP Photo: Jim Sulleu 28
Corbis: Archivo Iconografico, S.A. 15, Arte & Immagini srl 14, Bettmann 30, 43, Gianni Dagli Orti 12, Dallas Morning News/Sygma 23, Shelley Gazin 22, Greenpeace/Sygma 47, Bob Krist 41, Pandis Media/Sygma 25, Jeffrey L. Rotman 16, D.Ryan/Beaumont Enterprise/Sygma 21, Greg Smith/SABA front cover and 45, 48, David Turnley 29
Mary Evans Picture Library: 13
Getty Images: 18, Phillippe Diederich 8, Erik S. Lesser 31, Spencer Platt 32, 36, Mike Simons 10, US Navy 42, Stefan Zaklin 51
Moviestore Collection: 27
PA Photos: 20, 33/EPA 9t, c, b, 26, 34, 35, 37, 39, 40, 44, 46, 49, 50, Sean Dempsey 24
Rex Features Ltd: 19/SIPA Press 11, 17
Still Pictures: John Maier, Jr 38

CONTENTS

Gary's Story

In May 1981, Gary Graham went on a crime spree in Houston, Texas, USA. In a week he committed nine robberies, involving guns and the threat of violence. At his trial he was accused of murdering Bobby Grant Lambert. Graham pleaded guilty to the robberies, but denied murder. Despite flimsy evidence, Graham was convicted of murder and sentenced to death.

FROM THE START it was clear that Graham had not been well defended at his trial. The main evidence against him was provided by an eyewitness named Bernadine Skillern. However, she was the only one out of six witnesses who identified Graham as the killer. Furthermore, the incident took place at night, and Skillern only saw the killer fleetingly. Yet the defence attorney did not cross-examine her. Also, ballistics experts could not say with any certainty whether Graham's gun had fired the bullet responsible for the death or not.

In 1988, four witnesses came forward claiming that Graham had been with them on the night of the murder. An appeal was made against the guilty verdict, but it was turned down. Other holes were also found in the prosecution case. For example, two of the witnesses claimed the murderer was under 1.6 m tall; Graham was 1.78 m. In all, a total of 33 appeals were made against the verdict, and each one was rejected.

When Graham began his sentence he was a rebellious young man who frequently fought with his jailers. Over the years he became more resigned to his fate. He saw himself as a casualty in a war against injustice. When the

scheduled date of execution drew near, Graham's lawyers made a final appeal for clemency to George W Bush, then the state's governor. Bush took the advice of the Texas parole board, and turned down the appeal.

Graham's execution was to be carried out by lethal injection. On the day of the execution, Graham became angry and bitter once again. He had to be subdued by prison guards and carried into the execution room. He was covered in a sheet and restrained as he was injected with the poisonous drugs. He looked over towards one of his supporters, let out a slight groan, then died.

The family of Bobby Grant Lambert issued a statement afterwards saying that they were sorry for Graham's family. However, they felt that justice had been done.

The Death Penalty

Whether ethical or not, the death penalty is legal punishment in countries all over the world.

CHINA
China sentences more people to death than any other country. Here people are executed for crimes such as murder, robbery, rape, bomb-throwing, arson and sabotage. In 2002, it is believed that 1060 people were executed, though the real figure may be much higher.

IRAN
Iran had the second highest number of executions in 2002, with 113 people put to death. The death penalty is popular in this country and some newspapers have claimed that death sentences are imposed because judges are influenced by the opinion of the public.

UNITED STATES
The third highest number of executions in 2002 occurred in the USA, where 71 people were executed. Here the death penalty is imposed only for crimes involving murder. Capital punishment is legal in all but 12 states and the District of Columbia.

What Is Capital Punishment?

*Capital punishment is the execution, or killing, of a person as a punishment for committing a crime. The word **capital**, meaning the top of something, refers to a person's head; in the past people were often executed by severing their head from their body. Today, there are many different kinds of execution, including lethal injection, electrocution, gassing, hanging, shooting, beheading and stoning.*

CAPITAL PUNISHMENT has been used by societies throughout history. Today, the death sentence is most commonly used as a punishment for very serious crimes, such as murder, terrorism and rape. Whether or not an offence is judged to be a capital crime (a crime worthy of the death penalty) often depends on the culture or religion of a particular country.

Capital punishment is an issue that has stirred a great deal of debate in recent times. There are many opponents of the death penalty, as well as many others who believe that it is a just form of punishment. In this book we will look at the arguments for and against capital punishment. We will ask whether it is right for a government to order someone's death, and whether this acts as a deterrent to other potential murderers. We will also look at what life is like for those condemned to death.

Is capital punishment fair?

If people agree that capital punishment is just, they must then consider whether it is applied fairly. Does the justice system in a particular country always produce fair verdicts? Do innocent people sometimes get

The electric chair was a common form of execution in the USA during the 20th century. Today, however, only one state – Nebraska – still uses it.

Some countries use a firing squad in executions. Usually, a team of five executioners fire at the prisoner. One of them fires a blank, so the identity of the executioner is not known.

A suitable punishment?

'Life sentences too often are mere challenges for prisoners to escape, terrify law-abiding citizens and sometimes kill again... Even the toughest criminals become remarkably docile once separated from society by six feet of soil.'

Deroy Murdock, senior fellow with the Atlas Economic Research Foundation

'I have observed that it never does a boy much good to shoot him.'

President Abraham Lincoln, on Roswell McIntyre, sentenced to death for desertion

executed? And what about vulnerable groups such as the young, the old, pregnant women, foreigners, racial minorities or the mentally ill? Is it right for people in these groups to face capital punishment? These and many other questions will be discussed in the following chapters.

Has Capital Punishment Always Existed?

*Throughout history, governments have executed criminals. Some of the earliest societies believed that a government had the right to take revenge on behalf of the victim. This right is laid down in an ancient legal principle known as **lex talionis** ('law of retaliation'), which says 'an eye for an eye, a tooth for a tooth, a life for a life'.*

THE PRINCIPLE OF *lex talionis* appears as far back as the 18th century BC in the law code of Hammurabi, king of the Babylonians. Under this code, the death penalty was imposed for 25 different crimes. It also appears in Mosaic Law, the code of the Hebrew prophet and law-giver, Moses, who lived around the 13th century BC. Mosaic Law was regarded as the law of God, and it could be extremely harsh. If a sacrifice was made to any other god apart from 'the Lord', then that person should be 'utterly destroyed'.

This stone carving shows Hammurabi. During his reign, the death penalty was used for crimes such as telling lies, stealing from a temple and even mixing with criminals.

Who decided on the convictions of criminals?

In Europe in the early Middle Ages (AD 400–1100), the punishment of thieves and murderers was left to the family of the victim to decide. By the 1100s, people began to believe that serious crimes, such as robbery and murder, were not merely a matter for the victim, but were a crime against society as a whole. This belief lead to the executions of many criminals in front of the public who were able to see that punishment was being carried out and justice done.

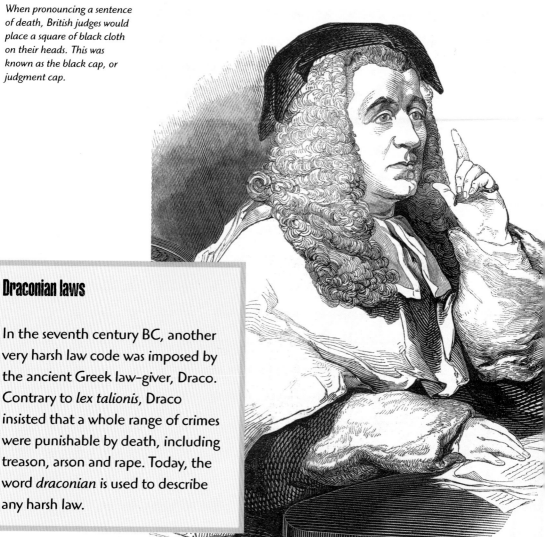

When pronouncing a sentence of death, British judges would place a square of black cloth on their heads. This was known as the black cap, or judgment cap.

Draconian laws

In the seventh century BC, another very harsh law code was imposed by the ancient Greek law-giver, Draco. Contrary to *lex talionis*, Draco insisted that a whole range of crimes were punishable by death, including treason, arson and rape. Today, the word *draconian* is used to describe any harsh law.

In the 15th and 16th centuries, religious divisions in Europe and executions for heresy (holding beliefs that go against the established faith) became commonplace. In the reign of Henry VIII of England (1509–1547), for example, an estimated 72 000 people were executed, many of them for 'religious crimes'. European settlers who settled in the New World took the death penalty with them. Laws regarding the death penalty varied from one American colony to another, and – after the formation of the USA – from one state to another.

Capital punishment remained widespread throughout the world until the 19th century, when, in Western Europe and in some states of the USA, it began to be replaced by other kinds of punishment, such as life imprisonment. The death penalty was reintroduced in the 20th century by authoritarian regimes such as Nazi Germany and Fascist Italy. Today, there is a global trend away from capital punishment. By 2003, it had been abolished in 76 countries, and a further 36 countries rarely used it.

How were people executed in the past?

The human imagination can be seen at its most cruel in the methods devised for executing criminals. Whereas, in recent times, efforts have been made to make the process of administering death relatively quick and painless, earlier societies appeared to take delight in inventing methods that could be painful and gruesome. Methods have included being stoned to death, burned alive, fed to wild animals or ripped apart by being tied to horses that were running in opposite directions.

In ancient Rome, murderers and traitors were hurled from a clifftop near the city known as the Tarpeian Rock. Those who killed their fathers were drowned in a sealed bag together with a dog, a cock, an ape and a viper.

Cruel forms of execution in ancient China included sawing the condemned in half or boiling them in oil. In Europe, offenders were sometimes hanged, drawn and quartered: hanged victims were taken down from the scaffold while still alive, disembowelled and

A particularly painful form of execution was crucifixion, where the condemned man was tied or nailed to a cross. According to the Bible, Jesus Christ was executed in this manner.

forced to watch their entrails being burned in front of them. They were then beheaded, and their bodies chopped into four pieces.

Were executions held in public?

Executions were seen as public events and were often attended by large crowds. Public executions were banned in England in 1868, but continued to take place in parts of the USA until the 1930s. In Guatemala, executions have even been broadcast on television.

Attitudes began to change in the 18th century, and more humane methods of execution were sought. During the French Revolution at the end of the 18th century, for example, the guillotine was developed. It was a mechanical beheading device that proved far more quick and efficient than the traditional executioner's axe. In 1890, the electric chair was used for the first time in New York state, and other states soon adopted this method, which was viewed as less cruel than hanging. In 1924, cyanide gas was introduced in Nevada as a more humane form of execution, and, in 1977, Oklahoma became the first state to adopt the lethal injection.

Traditional methods of execution, such as beheading and stoning, still persist in some countries around the world, including Saudi Arabia, Iran, Sudan and Nigeria. Public executions continue to be carried out in some 20 countries, although the practice has been condemned by the United Nations Human Rights Committee as 'incompatible with human dignity'.

In medieval times, public hangings drew large crowds, including families with children. Multiple hangings were common: the gallows at Tyburn in London could hang eight criminals at once.

Iron-Age executions

Tacitus (AD 56–c120), the Roman historian, tells of the punishments for crimes among the Iron-Age tribes in Germany: 'The mode of execution varies according to the offence. Traitors and deserters are hanged in trees: cowards, shirkers... are pressed down under a wicker hurdle into the slimy mud of a bog... offenders against the state should be made a public example of, whereas deeds of shame should be buried out of men's sight.'

Tacitus, The Germania, page 111

Why Are People Executed?

Capital punishment is usually reserved for the most serious offences, but what is a serious offence? In most countries, the worst crime of all is murder, and all countries with the death penalty will execute murderers. Some countries also regard terrorism, drug dealing, rape and blasphemy as offences worthy of the death penalty.

These people have been accused of drug smuggling and, if found guilty, could face the death penalty. Drug smuggling is punishable by death in 34 countries around the world.

DEBATE – Should capital punishment be used for crimes other than murder?

- Yes. Each country has the right to decide what constitutes a capital crime according to its own traditions, and it is not for others to judge them.

- No. People should not be executed for fighting against unjust regimes or disobeying unjust laws. Similarly, poor people must sometimes steal to survive, and it is not fair that they should die for this.

WHAT IS OR is not a capital crime depends very much on the type of government, and the culture and traditions of a particular country. In Iraq under Saddam Hussein, for example, the death penalty could be inflicted for evading military service. In Sri Lanka, it can be imposed for helping someone commit suicide or for dealing drugs. In Zambia, merely wounding someone in the course of a robbery can lead to capital punishment.

In certain Muslim countries, such as Sudan, Iran, Pakistan and Saudi Arabia, apostasy (rejection) of Islam, or blasphemy, are capital offences. In Egypt and Kuwait – countries that have suffered from terrorist attacks – terrorism carries a death sentence. And in at least 25 countries, financial crimes such as corruption, embezzlement (stealing company money), bribery, fraud, forgery, smuggling and theft are capital offences.

Some countries impose the death penalty for certain crimes retroactively (after the crime has been committed). Israel imposed a death sentence on Adolf Eichmann, the Nazi war criminal, even though the crimes he committed had occurred in Europe, before Israel had been founded. In Nigeria, people have been executed for drugs offences committed before the death penalty had been applied to these crimes.

The Shari'ah

All Muslims follow Islamic law, known as the *Shari'ah*, which is found in the Muslim holy book, the Qur'an. The *Shari'ah* defines how believers should behave. It also lays down suitable punishments for offences. Death is the accepted punishment for several *Hudud* crimes (crimes set down in the Qur'an that have fixed penalties). In Islamic countries such as Saudi Arabia and Sudan, the *Shari'ah* is enshrined in the nation's laws, and cases are tried in *Shari'ah* courts.

An armed policeman stands guard by the Temple of Hatshepsut in Egypt, the scene of a terrorist attack in 1997. The Egyptian government has imposed the death penalty for many forms of terrorism.

Is Capital Punishment Right Or Wrong?

The issue of capital punishment has stirred fierce debate among philosophers, campaigners and legal experts. The arguments, both for and against, are both moral and practical. The moral arguments are to do with personal feelings about the subject. The practical arguments are concerned with how the system works in practice.

SUPPORTERS OF THE death penalty argue that capital punishment is a just form of vengeance, expressing the anger of the victim's relatives and society in general, and reinforcing the moral code upon which society is based. They believe that a murderer has forfeited the right to his or her own life.

Opponents of capital punishment say that punishing murderers by killing them sends out the message that killing is not always wrong. Death penalty supporters reject this argument; if capital punishment teaches people to kill, they say, do prison sentences teach people that it's okay to hold someone against their will, and do fines teach that it's alright to steal? They say that this argument confuses killing the innocent with punishing the guilty. Abolitionists (those who wish to abolish the death penalty) believe that all people have a right to life, and that capital punishment

Sister Helen Prejean, a campaigner against the death penalty, wrote the influential book, Dead Man Walking (1994), which opened many people's eyes to the dreadful existence of prisoners in the USA on death row.

Timothy McVeigh was executed in June 2001. He was found guilty of the bomb attack on the federal building in Oklahoma City, USA, in April 1995.

DEBATE – Do people who commit murder forfeit their own right to life?

* Yes. Anyone who has deliberately taken the life of another has violated that person's right to life. Justice demands that they receive the same treatment as their victim.

* No. Killing a murderer does not bring the victim back to life. It achieves nothing but the death of yet another person.

violates this right and is inhuman and degrading. In answer to this, Ed Koch, former mayor of New York City and supporter of the death penalty, said, 'It is by exacting the highest penalty for the taking of human life that we affirm the highest value of life'.

What do Jews and Christians think about capital punishment?

Historically, both Jews and Christians have justified capital punishment by the Old Testament passage, 'Whosoever sheddeth man's blood, by man shall his blood be shed' (*Genesis* 9:6). However, there are also passages in the Bible that require the death penalty for actions such as sex before marriage, adultery, homosexuality and working on the Sabbath (holy day). Few Jews and

Christians today believe that these passages have much relevance in modern society.

Today, there is no general agreement among Jews or Christians on the morality of capital punishment. During the second half of the 20th century, a number of religious leaders – especially Jews and Roman Catholics – campaigned against the death penalty. Capital punishment was abolished by the Jewish state of Israel for all offences except treason and crimes against humanity, and Pope John Paul II condemned it as 'cruel and unnecessary'.

Lucille McLauchlan, along with fellow nurse Deborah Parry, was found guilty of murder in Saudi Arabia. The victim's family wanted them executed, but the Saudi king commuted their sentences.

What about the rights of victims?

Justice for victims is often given as a major reason for the death penalty. But what do the families of murder victims think about the death penalty? Many believe that their feelings and the rights of their dead relative are overlooked in the general debate over how the murderer should be punished. In the USA, several groups have been formed by relatives of murder victims, including Justice for All and Citizens Against Homicide. These groups offer support and advice, for example on how to obtain compensation for their loss, and how to campaign to keep the murderer of their relative in prison. Some people choose to attend the execution of their relative's murderer. This may help to bring a sense of closure to their suffering.

Some victims' families do not support capital punishment. They may express a wish that their loss should not be used as a reason for another family's bereavement. Others have said that execution is too quick and easy a punishment, and believe that life imprisonment will give the murderer more time to think about and repent his or her actions. Still others have expressed forgiveness for the murderer. One American victim group, called Murder Victims' Families for Reconciliation (MVFR), actively campaigns against the death penalty.

What are the victims' rights in Islamic countries?

In Islamic countries, the families of murder victims often get to decide on the punishment of their relative's killer. According to the *Shari'ah*, murder is not a *Hudud* crime, meaning that it does not carry a fixed penalty as laid down in the Qur'an. The penalty for premeditated (preplanned) murder given by the *Shari'ah* courts is usually death, but it is up to the victim's family to decide whether the sentence is carried out or not. They may ask for *Qisas*, or retaliation, which means death for a

convicted murderer, or they may choose to pardon the murderer and accept 'blood money' – financial compensation for the loss. This is called *Diya*. The Qur'an encourages victims' families to choose *Diya*, promising the forgiveness of sins to those who extend forgiveness to murderers. Executions may be delayed for many years if, for example, the heirs of a victim are not yet old enough to make their decision. *Diya* can sometimes take place on the very day of execution. In June 2001, a 20-year-old Yemeni man's life was spared by the victim's father as the executioner was raising his sword to behead him.

MVFR mission statement

'Our opposition to the death penalty is rooted in our direct experience of loss and our refusal to respond to that loss with a quest for more killing. Executions are not what will help us heal.'

Ross Byrd is the son of James Byrd Jr, who was killed in Texas in 1998 by John W King. Ross spoke out against the death penalty that had been served on his father's killer.

An accused person talks with his legal counsel. Many countries, such as the USA, Thailand and Turkey, offer free legal representation to defendants who cannot afford a lawyer.

What are the practical arguments for and against capital punishment?

Aside from the moral issues, there is also a debate about how well the death penalty works in practice. These include the following questions: Is it possible to administer a system of capital punishment in a way that is just and fair? Are innocent people sometimes executed? Does capital punishment deter others from committing murder? Does it make society safer?

Is the death penalty always fairly applied?

It has been claimed that the implementation of the death penalty is unfair to people on low incomes. Poor people make up the vast majority of prisoners on death row in the United States. They cannot afford to hire their own lawyers and must depend on public defenders of variable quality. In some states, such as Alabama, there is no public defender system, and the court will assign an attorney to low-income defendants from a pool of local lawyers. These lawyers are usually poorly paid and often lack any significant experience in capital punishment cases. This may lead to a failure to call important witnesses or to present evidence that could mean the difference between life and death for the defendant.

Poor person's punishment

'The death penalty is a poor person's issue. Always remember that: after all the rhetoric that goes on in the legislative assemblies, in the end... it is the poor who are selected to die in this country.'

Sister Helen Prejean, Sisters of St Joseph, a campaigner against the death penalty

Racial executions

US Death Row inmates executed between January 1976 and July 2003

Race of defendant	Number executed	Percentage of total
White	495	57%
Black	298	34%
Hispanic	57	7%
Other	20	2%

Betty Lou Beets was one of the few women to be executed in the USA when she was killed by lethal injection in February 2000, having been found guilty of mudering her husband.

Sometimes racial prejudice can be a factor motivating juries on capital cases, leading to the execution of ethnic minorities in higher than average numbers. Research in the USA has shown that in capital cases where the defendant was black and the victim white, conviction rates varied according to the racial make-up of the jury. When there were four or fewer white males on the jury in a case involving a black defendant and a white victim, 30 per cent of juries opted for the death penalty. But when there were five or more white men on the jury, 70 per cent sentenced to death. Evidence also suggests that sentences vary according to the ethnic origin of the victim. Some 80 per cent of prisoners executed in the USA since 1977 were convicted of killing a white victim, although whites make up only about half of all murder victims.

Are different sexes treated differently?

Some people point to a discrepancy in the conviction rates between the sexes. In 2003, there were just 48 women on death row in the USA, making up a mere 1.5 per cent of the total number of prisoners awaiting execution. And since 1962, just ten women have been executed in the USA, compared with 870 men executed since 1976. Certain countries even exclude women from the death penalty. These include Belarus, Mongolia, Uzbekistan, Cuba and Russia. Critics argue that it is unfair to treat convicted criminals differently just on the basis of their gender.

The Birmingham Six celebrate their release. If Britain had had the death penalty, they would probably have been executed.

Do innocent people get executed?

Criminal justice systems sometimes make mistakes, and there are many cases of people convicted of crimes who have later been proved innocent. One famous example of this is the case of the Birmingham Six, a group of six men who spent 16 years in prison in the UK charged with causing a bomb explosion in 1974. They were later freed when evidence used in the trial against them was discredited. People who have spent time in prison for crimes they did not commit are justifiably angry about their ordeal. It is even worse for the families of innocent people who have been wrongly accused and executed.

Miscarriages of justice are most likely to occur when there is government or media pressure on the police and the justice system to find and convict an offender. This might happen following a particularly awful crime that has aroused a lot of public anger. Or it might happen after a government crackdown on crime, such as the 'war on crime' in Russia in 1995–1996. During this period, the proportion of people executed who were later found to be innocent rose from 15 per cent to 30 per cent.

Do appeals work?

In the USA, 111 people in 25 states were released from death row between 1976 and July 2003, as new evidence had emerged to prove their innocence. Supporters of the death penalty argue that these figures show that the appeals process works, and the innocent are generally saved from execution. However, many of these cases were overturned not because of the appeals process, but thanks to the confessions of

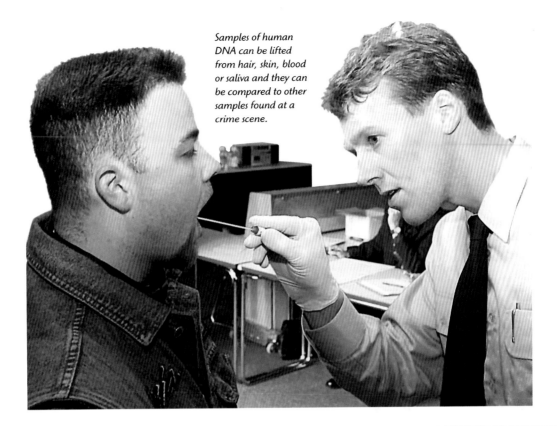

Samples of human DNA can be lifted from hair, skin, blood or saliva and they can be compared to other samples found at a crime scene.

other criminals, scientific techniques or the efforts of campaigners working outside the justice system.

Other death-penalty supporters cast doubt on the statistics. They say there should be a distinction made between 'legal innocence' and 'actual innocence'. They claim the figure of '111' prisoners released includes many whose guilty verdict was overturned thanks simply to a legal technicality.

It is very difficult to calculate how many innocent people in the USA may have been executed since 1976, since US courts do not generally review cases once the defendant is dead. However, there are several examples of executed people with strong claims of innocence. For example, new DNA evidence has thrown doubt on the rape and murder conviction of Joseph O'Dell, who was executed in 1997.

DNA testing

DNA testing is a method of identifying a person by analysing their DNA, a molecule found in every cell of every living thing that is unique to that individual. There is a campaign in the USA to make DNA testing available to all death-row inmates who are protesting their innocence. In 2001, 17 states passed laws to allow this to happen. By removing any doubt from a conviction, DNA testing could rob abolitionists of one of their key arguments against the death penalty: the possibility of innocence.

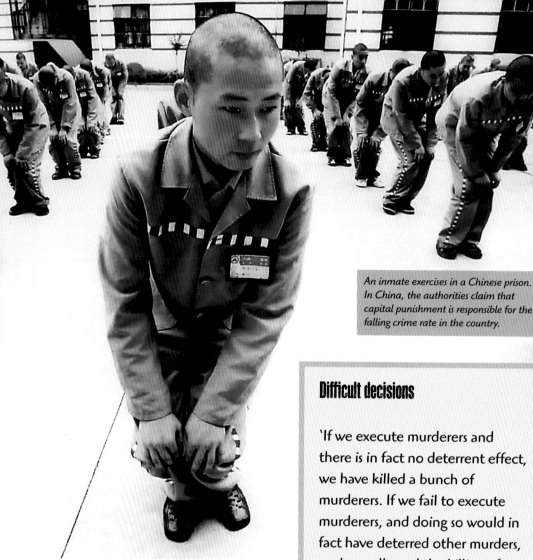

An inmate exercises in a Chinese prison. In China, the authorities claim that capital punishment is responsible for the falling crime rate in the country.

Difficult decisions

'If we execute murderers and there is in fact no deterrent effect, we have killed a bunch of murderers. If we fail to execute murderers, and doing so would in fact have deterred other murders, we have allowed the killing of a bunch of innocent victims. I would much rather risk the former. This, to me, is not a tough call.'

John McAdams, Marquette University, Department of Political Science

How can criminal justice systems be made fairer?

One way of reducing the number of executions of innocent people is to ensure that the criminal justice system observes the rights of the defendant to a fair trial. The United Nations (an organisation of countries formed after World War II) has sought to establish a set of standards that all countries with the death penalty should abide by. These include the following: defendants should be informed of the nature of the charge against them and be given enough time to prepare a defence; defendants should be given adequate legal representation, and be able to get hold of and examine witnesses to help their case; and they should expect a fair trial with an unbiased jury, and have the right to appeal against the verdict.

Many countries with the death penalty fall far short of these standards. In Saudi Arabia, trials have taken place in which the defendant has no legal representation at all. The right to prepare a defence and to a fair trial and the right of appeal have all been denied on many occasions in China, where executions have sometimes been carried out between six and eight days after an arrest. In Iran, there have been reports of drug offenders being refused both legal representation and the right of appeal.

Is the death penalty a deterrent?

One of the major practical arguments in favour of capital punishment is that it deters others from murder. It is assumed that people are less likely to commit murder if they know that they may die themselves if they are caught. Abolitionists reject the deterrence argument. They claim that most murders are not planned in advance by rational people who consider the consequences of their actions. Murderers are often people who have found it difficult to fit into normal society. Their crimes are usually the result of thoughtless outbursts of anger or fear. Supporters argue that the low number of rational, calculating killers is perhaps explained by the presence of the death penalty.

Hollywood typically views a murderer as a cold, calculating killer, such as Hannibal Lector from the film Silence of the Lambs. *But this kind of murderer is actually very rare.*

Death penalty supporters argue that a multiple killer, such as Jack Henry Abbott, would have been prevented from killing again if he had been executed.

Is the deterrent argument supported by statistics?

Statistical evidence has been used both for and against the deterrent argument. Death penalty supporters point to the dramatic rise in murders in the USA during and just after the period 1967–1976, when there was a national moratorium (a formal halt) on executions. Between 1966 and 1980, executions in the USA averaged less than one every four years, and the murder rate rose from 5.6 to 10.2 per 100 000 people. From 1995 to 2000, US executions averaged 71 per year. By 1999, the murder rate had fallen to 5.7 per 100 000, its lowest level since 1966.

There are also instances in which the murder rate has not risen after a country has abolished the death penalty. In some cases the murder rate has fallen. Capital punishment was abolished in Canada in 1976 and the murder rate (per 100 000) fell from 3.09 in 1975 to 1.76 in 1999.

Some capital punishment supporters completely reject the deterrence argument, basing their support entirely on the fact that the death penalty punishes the guilty. They say that the deterrent argument would be a very unfair reason to support the death penalty, since it implies that people are killed not because they deserve it, but for the good of society. As the Christian writer, CS Lewis explains, 'If deterrence is all that matters, the execution of an innocent man, provided the public think him guilty, would be fully justified.'

Does the death penalty make us safer?

One obvious point often made by death-penalty supporters is that an executed killer cannot one day escape from prison, or be set free, to kill or injure again. It is therefore true to say that capital punishment contributes to the safety of our society. However, it is generally very rare for killers, once released, to kill again. Since the 1970s, there have only been around ten documented cases in the USA of murderers killing someone else after having been set free.

What is the cost of the death penalty?

On the face of it, the death penalty would appear to be a way of saving the taxpaying public the cost of keeping someone in prison for life. After a person is executed, there are no further costs to the state. However, research has shown that – in the USA at least – the death penalty system is actually more expensive to administer than life imprisonment. This is because of the combined costs of funding appeals and keeping death-row inmates in prison for years, even decades, while the appeals process takes place. A 2003 study showed that each death penalty case in Texas cost the taxpayer about US$2.3 million more than a case resulting in life imprisonment without parole.

DEBATE - Is a miscarriage of justice a good reason for abolishing the death penalty?

- Yes. The statistics show that justice systems are not infallible, and they probably never will be. A prison inmate at least has the opportunity to clear his or her name eventually. An executed innocent can never be given another chance.

- No. A few innocents may have to die in order to maintain a system that will deter future would-be murderers from killing a far greater number of innocent people.

Life imprisonment convicts work in a prison workshop. Some death penalty abolitionists argue that prisoners should be able to earn money to pay for part of their imprisonment.

Is There A Movement To Abolish Capital Punishment?

The modern movement to abolish capital punishment dates from the 18th century. In 1764, the Italian scholar Cesare Beccaria published **On Crimes and Punishments,** *which proposed the abolition of the death penalty. Beccaria believed that it was inhumane and ineffective and that it gave legitimacy to killing.*

Cesare Beccaria argued that the law is morally inconsistent by killing people for killing people.

IN THE 1780s, Beccaria's ideas were taken up by the rulers of Russia, Austria and Tuscany, where capital punishment was suspended for several years. The abolitionist movement grew in Europe and the United States, and in 1794, Pennsylvania became the first state in the USA to abolish capital punishment for all crimes but murder. In 1861, Michigan became the first American state – and the first territory anywhere in the world – to abolish capital punishment for all crimes. It was soon followed by Rhode Island and Wisconsin. In 1863, Venezuela became the first country to abolish capital punishment for all crimes.

European states soon began to follow this example. In 1861, England abandoned capital punishment for all crimes except murder, and by 1925, Portugal, the Netherlands, Norway, Sweden, Italy, Romania, Austria and Switzerland had abolished the death penalty for all peacetime crimes. A similar movement occurred among several newly independent South American states, including Brazil, Colombia, Uruguay and Argentina.

Anti-death penalty campaigners on vigil in the USA.

However, the movement towards abolition was not a one-way process. Many European and South American countries fell under authoritarian regimes in the 1930s and 1940s, which reimposed capital punishment. By 1965, 25 countries had abolished the death penalty for murder, and 11 of these had abolished it for all crimes.

How many abolitionist countries are there?

Between 1965 and 2003, the number of abolitionist countries grew from 25 to 91. A further 21 countries have not executed anyone for a number of years and are regarded as abolitionist in practice. In 1965, there were two abolitionist countries outside Europe and Central and South America. By 2003, 11 countries from Africa were on the list, and another 11 from the Pacific islands.

Public murder

'It seems to me absurd that the laws, which are an expression of the public will, which detest and punish homicide, should themselves commit it, and that to deter citizens from murder they order a public one.'

Cesare Beccaria, On Crimes and Punishments

There have been a few formerly abolitionist countries that have brought back capital punishment, including Papua New Guinea (abolished 1975 and reinstated 1991) and the Philippines (abolished 1987 and reinstated 1993). Nevertheless, the trend remains in the direction of abolition.

The security council of the United Nations in session. The UN has passed resolutions aimed at encouraging countries to abolish the death penalty.

Is the United Nations against capital punishment?

During the second half of the 20th century, there was a remarkable increase in the number of abolitionist countries. One of the main reasons for this was the success of those opposed to the death penalty in making capital punishment an international human rights issue, rather than a matter for each country to decide on for themselves.

The process began with the 'Universal Declaration of Human Rights' passed by the United Nations (UN) in 1948. Although this did not specifically condemn capital punishment, it did contain several clauses that could be interpreted as being against the death penalty. Article three affirmed that everyone had a right to life, and Article five declared that no one should face 'cruel, inhuman or degrading... punishment'. This marked a turning point in the attitudes of many governments; of the 76 countries that were abolitionist for all crimes in 2003, 68 abolished the death penalty after 1948, including the UK.

In 1966, the UN adopted an agreement called the International Covenant on Civil and Political Rights (ICCPR). Again, capital punishment was not specifically banned, but it did proclaim that 'every human being has the right to life' and that 'no one shall be arbitrarily deprived of his life'. Article six of the ICCPR said that capital punishment should be restricted to 'the most serious of crimes'.

In 1971, the UN took its first step towards declaring the abolition of the death penalty as a universal goal. The organisation passed a resolution calling for a restriction in the number of crimes for which the death penalty could be imposed, with a view to the eventual abolition of capital punishment.

The UN passed a further resolution in 1989 requiring signatories to abolish capital punishment except in time of war, and banning any state from reestablishing the death penalty after having abolished it. By 2003, a total of 49 countries had ratified this agreement (meaning they had adopted it as law), and a further seven had signed but not yet ratified it.

Have any countries refused to sign?

One of the main obstacles faced by those who wish to impose a universal ban on capital punishment is that many countries see it as an attempt by the international community to interfere with their own internal laws and customs. Countries such as Egypt, Singapore and Saudi Arabia regularly refuse to sign UN resolutions on the death penalty, or else introduce amendments to them that preserve the rights of individual countries to choose their own justice systems without outside interference.

Derek Bentley was hanged in the UK in January 1953 for the murder of a policeman. His conviction was influential in the abolition of the death penalty in the country.

Right to choose

'We recognise that many countries have abolished the death penalty under their domestic laws and that a number of countries have accepted treaty obligations to that effect, and we respect their decision to do so. However, we believe that in democratic societies the criminal justice system... should reflect the will of the people freely expressed and appropriately implemented through their elected representatives.'

The US government's reply to a UN survey in 2000

What other international organisations are against capital punishment?

The Council of Europe – an organisation of European countries that seeks to protect human rights – was inspired by the UN's 1971 call to abolish the death penalty, and in 1983 it adopted a resolution requiring the abolition of capital punishment in peacetime. By 2003, this had been ratified by 41 countries and signed by four. In early 2003, the Council of Europe took the final step towards complete abolition. An agreement was passed that declared the death penalty should be banned in all circumstances, both during war and peacetime. By July 2003, this had been ratified by 17 states, and signed by 24.

The Council of Europe's stand had a powerful effect on countries in central and eastern Europe hoping to join the European Union (EU). The Council established as a condition of their membership that they suspend

Abdullah Ocalan, the Kurdish rebel leader, was sentenced to death by Turkey in June 1999. To avoid damaging the country's chances of joining the EU, the sentence was commuted to life imprisonment.

DEBATE – Should a country's citizen be sent back to another country where he committed a crime, even though he may face the death penalty?

- No. The offender's country of origin has a duty to protect its citizens from being executed by a foreign government.

- Yes. A country has the right to try and, if necessary, execute someone who breaks its laws, whatever their country of origin. Otherwise the victims of the crime will be unable to see that justice has been done.

executions and move towards complete abolition. This prompted several, including the Czech Republic, Hungary, Romania, Slovakia and Slovenia, to abolish the death penalty, and has led to problems for Turkey, which has tried to become a member.

The Organisation of American States (OAS) – an organisation of countries in North and South America – adopted an agreement in 1990 that called on states to abstain from using the death penalty. However, it did not insist that they repeal the laws permitting its use. By 2003, eight countries (all from South and Central America) had ratified the agreement, and one (Chile) had signed it.

Extradition Cases

Extradition is the handing over by a government of somebody accused of a crime in a different country for trial and punishment there. In 1989, the European Court of Human Rights prohibited the extradition to the US state of Virginia of a suspect accused of a capital offence. The court decided he would face 'inhuman/degrading treatment or punishment', which went against the European Convention on Human Rights. This developed into a firm policy of the European Union in 2000.

Mohamed Rashed Daoud Owhali was deported by South Africa to the USA to stand trial for the bombing of the US embassy in Nairobi. The South African court was criticised because it did not obtain assurances from the USA that the suspect would not be executed.

Do Vulnerable People Get Executed?

Many people have argued that there are certain people who should not be subjected to the death penalty. These include young people, elderly people, pregnant women, new mothers, the mentally ill, the mentally retarded and foreign nationals. In this chapter we will look at whether members of these groups ever face execution.

Pervez Musharaf, the President of Pakistan, who commuted the death sentences of 100 juveniles on death row to life imprisonment in December 2001.

SOME BELIEVE that murder should be punished by death, and that the age of the murderer is not relevant. They say that any minimum age for those who may face capital punishment would be arbitrary (based on personal feelings, not facts). However, many others believe that young people form a separate category, because they are less mature, and therefore less responsible for their actions. They point out that many young murderers are themselves victims of abuse, and perhaps they should be helped rather than executed.

The international community is generally in favour of banning the execution of the young. In 1984, the UN passed a resolution stating that persons below 18 years of age at the time a crime was committed should not be sentenced to death. This commitment was confirmed by the Convention of the Rights of the Child, passed by the UN in November 1989, which has been ratified by every member nation except the USA. Since 1990, a number of nations have passed laws banning the execution of young people, including Yemen, China, Sudan and Thailand. In 2001,

Juvenile Chinese prisoners receive a lecture. The country banned the death penalty for young people in 1997.

Pakistan commuted (reduced) the death sentences on nearly 100 juveniles to life imprisonment.

What is the minimum age in the USA?

In the USA, the minimum age for the death penalty varies from state to state. In 1988, the US Supreme Court ruled that it was unconstitutional to impose the death penalty on people under the age of 16 at the time of the offence, but it left it up to individual state legislatures to rule on cases involving 16 to 18 year olds. By March 2002, 13 states had set a minimum age of 18; four set it at 17; 12 at 16; and seven did not specify an age.

Uncivilised executions

'In my view, it's just not proper in a civilised society for the state to be in the business of executing children or those who are mentally retarded.'

Senator Greer of Tennessee, 12 April 1990.

In Tennessee, since 1984, people under the age of 18 cannot face the death penalty.

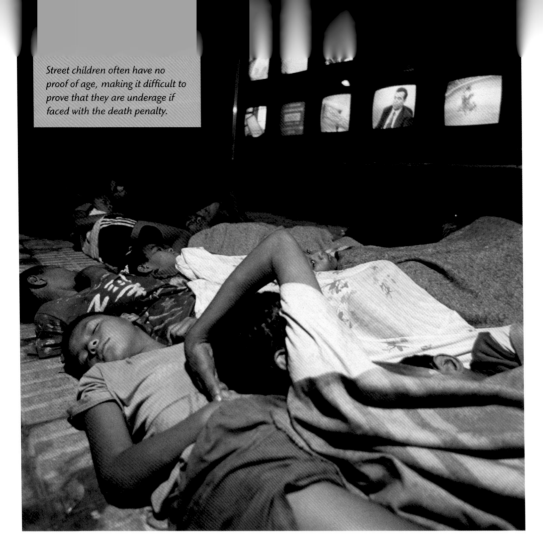

Street children often have no proof of age, making it difficult to prove that they are underage if faced with the death penalty.

Which countries continue to execute young people?

Despite having ratified international treaties banning this practice, certain countries continue to execute under 18s, or people who committed crimes when under 18. In some cases, the minimum age is fixed as low as 16. In Malaysia, there is no legal distinction made between adults and minors, and people under 16 can be executed. In India, a boy who was 15 at the time of the offence, was executed in 2001. In countries like the Philippines and Brazil, where poor street children often have no legal proof of age, it is difficult to be sure whether juveniles are being executed or not.

According to Amnesty International, there have been 20 documented executions of child offenders in five countries since 1994: the Democratic Republic of Congo, Iran, Nigeria, Pakistan and the USA. Some 13 of these executions took place in the USA.

Are pregnant women or new mothers executed?

Pregnant women charged with capital crimes are not automatically excluded from the death penalty in every country of the world. However, there have been no recent reports of pregnant women being executed, although a death sentence was imposed on one in the Democratic Republic of Congo in 1998.

New mothers are also not generally executed. Some countries wait for the child to be born and weaned before carrying out the sentence. Other countries, such as Kuwait, commute the sentence to life imprisonment. However, 16 countries, including Egypt, Japan, South Korea and Turkey, have informed the UN that they could not in all cases exempt new mothers from the death penalty. Several set a period, ranging from two months (Egypt) to two years (Yemen) after the baby is born, before the execution can be carried out.

Do old people face capital punishment?

The argument against the death penalty for young people – that they are less responsible for their actions – is not so easily applied to the elderly, unless it can be proved that they are suffering from senility (a loss of mental powers occurring in later life). Nevertheless, the UN has urged its member states to establish a maximum age beyond which people cannot be sentenced to death. Only a few countries have done this. The maximum age in the Philippines and Sudan is 70; in Kazakhstan and Russia it is 65; while in Mongolia, Guatemala and Mexico (for military offences) it is 60.

Amina Lawal with her baby.

The Case of Amina Lawal

As an unmarried woman, Amina Lawal became pregnant. Under the shari'ah-based laws that operate in the northern states of Nigeria where Amina lives, pregnancy outside of marriage is seen as evidence of adultery. In March 2002, Amina was sentenced to death by stoning. The man named as father of the baby girl denied having sex with Amina and was released. Human rights groups appealed against Amina's sentence, but in August 2002, the shari'ah court of appeal upheld (confirmed) the sentence. In September 2003, Amina won another appeal against the death sentence.

John Paul Penry has the mind of a child, but was nevertheless sentenced to death in Texas in 1980 for the rape and murder of Pamela Carpenter. He remains on death row today.

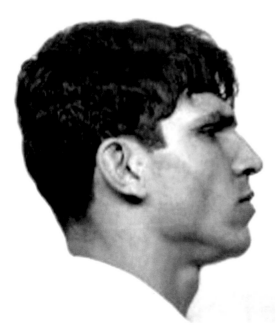

DEBATE – Should mentally ill criminals be treated any differently from other criminals?

- Yes. A person cannot be held responsible if they are unable to control their actions.
- No. What matters is the fact that the crime was committed, not the state of the person's mental health.

Do mentally ill people receive death sentences?

In all countries that have the death penalty allowances are made for people who are mentally ill. Many people believe that if someone is unable to control their actions due to mental illness, then they should not be held responsible for them. The problem is that the issue is not always black and white; there are many different forms and degrees of mental illness, and judging whether a person should or should not be held responsible for a crime can be subjective (based on a person's feelings, not facts).

It may depend on a number of factors, including the defendant's mental state at the time he or she is examined by a psychiatrist, the views of the particular psychiatrist, the attitude of the jury and the nature of the crime. Situations can become more complicated when psychiatrists appear as witnesses for both the prosecution and the defence and each present a different view of the defendant's mental state.

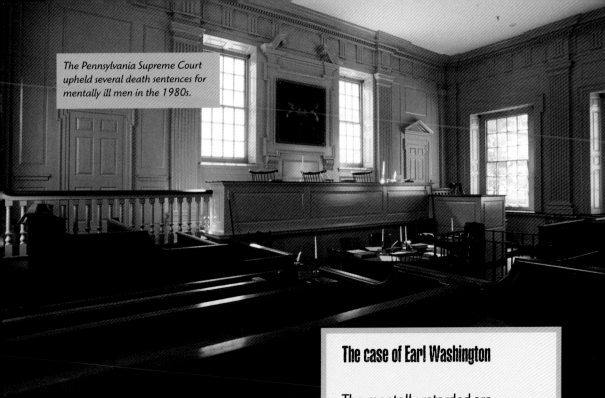

The Pennsylvania Supreme Court upheld several death sentences for mentally ill men in the 1980s.

In many countries, prisoners who become mentally ill after sentencing to death can still face execution, although it is often delayed until they are judged to have recovered. This places psychiatrists in the awkward position of knowing that the successful treatment of a patient may result in his or her execution.

Are the mentally retarded ever executed?

Mental retardation is a lifelong condition of impaired or incomplete mental development. In most countries, the mentally retarded are not executed unless they are judged to be able to control their actions. One exception is the USA, where it has been estimated that around 44 mentally retarded prisoners were executed between 1984 and 2001. In June 2002, the US Supreme Court ruled that executing the mentally retarded violated (broke) the eighth amendment to the constitution, amounting to a 'cruel and unusual punishment', and it has now been banned throughout the USA.

The case of Earl Washington

The mentally retarded are particularly vulnerable once they have entered the criminal justice system, as they are less likely to understand their rights and may be eager to please their interrogators by confessing. Earl Washington had an IQ of between 57 and 69. He was convicted of raping and murdering a young woman in Culpeper, Virginia, in 1982, on the evidence of a confession he made to police. It is not certain that all members of the jury were aware of how mentally retarded he was. Some 16 years after being sentenced to death, a DNA test proved his innocence. At one point he came within three days of execution.

Prisoners held by the USA at Camp X-Ray, Guantanamo Bay, Cuba, include foreign nationals who have been threatened with the death penalty.

Soldiers and the death penalty

Crimes committed by soldiers are usually dealt with in a different way than civilian crimes, especially in wartime. Soldiers are usually tried in military courts and judged by senior officers. In some cases they lack the normal rights and protections granted to civilian defendants. In Uganda in March 2003, three soldiers of the Uganda People's Defence Force were sentenced to death by firing squad for murder. The trial lasted just two days, during which time they had no legal representation. They were given no right to appeal and were executed about an hour after the sentence was passed.

Are foreign nationals ever executed?

Foreigners accused of capital crimes can be particularly vulnerable if they do not speak or understand the language spoken by their police interrogators or by those who cross-examine (question) them in court. There have been reports that migrant workers involved in capital cases in some Middle Eastern countries have not been provided with translations of courtroom proceedings.

Under international law, foreign nationals accused of a crime have the right to consular assistance (help from a government official from the defendant's country who is based in the country where he or she is being tried). Several foreign nationals have been executed in the USA without having been informed of this right, including Karl and Walter LaGrand, German citizens executed for murder in 1999.

Are people executed during wartime?

Many countries that do not have the death penalty in peacetime reserve the right to use it in time of war when the survival of the country is at stake. The death penalty is seen as a useful means of punishing 'enemies of the state', such as spies and saboteurs, and a way of deterring others from these activities. The UN resolutions seeking to ban the death penalty (see pages 32–33) do not apply to wartime situations.

Some governments try to widen the definition of 'enemies of the state' to justify executing prisoners of war (ordinary soldiers captured during battle). The Geneva Convention (1949), which has been ratified by almost every UN member state, is concerned with treatment of prisoners of war. In article three it prohibits violence or cruel treatment towards prisoners of war. It states that executions can only be carried out after sentencing by a 'regularly constituted court affording all the judicial guarantees which are recognised as indispensable by civilised peoples.'

> **DEBATE – Is it justifiable to execute people who threaten the security of a country during a national crisis, such as war?**
>
> * Yes. It is worth destroying one life to prevent thousands from dying in the event of a military attack.
> * No. Every individual has a right to life, whether a country is at war or not.

A group of African-American soldiers pictured during World War II. During World War II, 79% of executed US soldiers were African-American, though they made up less than 10% of the army.

What Is It Like For Prisoners Living Under A Death Sentence?

Waiting to be executed is a stressful experience. Psychological studies carried out on death row prisoners have shown high levels of frustration, fear and loneliness that are similar to the feelings experienced by the terminally ill. But for death row prisoners, the effects are made worse by the often severe conditions they live in.

In China, death row prisoners are usually kept handcuffed and with their feet in shackles for the entire period from sentencing to execution. This is typically around 40 days.

PRISONERS MIGHT HAVE to spend a long time waiting to be executed. Because of the length of the appeals process in the USA, the period between sentencing and execution can take many years. Gary Graham (see pages 8–9), for example, had to wait 19 years to be executed (in June 2000) for a crime he committed when he was 17 years old. It is not only the prisoners who suffer, but also their families, who may find it hard to remain positive and supportive over such long periods. Sometimes the families of victims also suffer, as they are unable to achieve a sense of closure on their own bereavement until the killer of their loved one has been executed.

Prisoners in other countries can also face long delays before execution. In Saudi Arabia, those convicted of murder must often wait until the victim's son has reached maturity, which can be up to 15 years, before their fate is known.

US prisoners often spend many years on death row. Since the 1980s, US courts have attempted to speed up executions by rejecting what they regard as excessive appeals, and laying down strict time limits by which appeals must be lodged.

Willie Turner's story

Willie Turner, who spent 17 years on death row in Virginia until his execution in May 1995, said this about his experience: 'It's the unending, uninterrupted immersion in death that wears on you so much. It's the parade of friends and acquaintances who leave for the death house and never come back, while your own desperate and lonely time drains away... It's watching yourself die over the years in the eyes of family and friends... I've spent over 5000 days on death row. Not a single waking hour of any of those days has gone by without me thinking about my date with the executioner.'

In Malaysia, one man had to wait from 1988 to 2000 before being executed, while in Zambia, prisoners can live under sentence of death for up to 25 years. However, the country with the worst record for keeping prisoners on death row the longest is Japan, where some prisoners have been waiting for over 30 years to be executed. In Japan, Belarus and Taiwan, the wait is made harder to bear because prisoners are not told exactly when they will be executed.

These prisoners are waiting to go into a Revolutionary Court in Iran where they will be offered no right of appeal if they are found guilty.

Ken Saro-Wiwa

The Nigerian human rights activist, Ken Saro-Wiwa, campaigned on behalf of the Ogoni people. He was arrested in 1994 and was held without charge for nine months before facing trial for the murder of four Ogoni leaders. Human rights groups claimed these were false charges. On 31 October 1995, he was sentenced to death by a military court. He was given no right of appeal, and was hanged just ten days later, despite worldwide protests.

Is there a right of appeal?

Under international law, all prisoners sentenced to death have the right to appeal against their sentence to a court of higher jurisdiction (legal authority). Almost all countries claim to observe this right, with the exception of the Revolutionary Courts in Iran and Libya, as well as military courts in several African countries.

Most countries that retain the death penalty offer a fixed period between sentencing and execution for appeals to be lodged. This period varies from country to country. In Madagascar, Chad and Yugoslavia, for example, it is just three days; Armenia, Bangladesh and Turkey allow a week; in China it is ten days; while in Bahrain, Lesotho, Rwanda, Syria and Thailand, it is 30 days or more. In the US state of Texas, defendants have 30 days following their conviction to present new evidence in their defence, otherwise they lose their right of appeal.

So although most countries offer the right of appeal, in many cases this is not worth a great deal, since the defendant's lawyers are not given enough time to search for and present evidence in defence of their client. Three or even 30 days is not much time to hunt for new witnesses or to locate physical evidence in support of a case.

Do people with death sentences ever receive clemency?

Many countries with the death penalty allow prisoners to seek clemency, or a reprieve, in which case their sentence is commuted (reduced) to a lesser penalty, such as life imprisonment. This may occur because there is some doubt about the defendant's guilt, or because the government, for whatever reason, decides it wants to show mercy.

In Thailand, an appeal for clemency can be made to the king within 60 days of sentencing, and he will decide whether or not to offer a pardon. Between 1994 and 1998, 133 Thai prisoners appealed to the king, and 50 were pardoned.

In 14 US states, the governor alone has the power to offer clemency, and in 11 states, he must decide only after hearing the recommendation of the Pardons Board or Advisory Group. In the case of federal prisoners, only the US president can grant clemency. Since 1976, 223 death row inmates in the USA have been granted clemency. Reasons for these include doubts about guilt or the personal feelings of a particular governor about the death penalty process.

Ken Saro-Wiwa used his popularity as an author to speak out against the military regime in Nigeria.

What are conditions like on death row?

Countries vary in the treatment of prisoners awaiting execution, but generally speaking conditions are less comfortable than those experienced by other prisoners. In Japan, death row inmates are often kept in manacles (handcuffs) for long periods, and visiting times for families and lawyers are severely restricted. In China, prisoners have both their hands and feet shackled, but death-row conditions are not a major concern in this country, where death sentences are carried out relatively quickly.

In Zambia, prisoners with death sentences face severe overcrowding, with up to six men held in cells approximately 3m by 2m. According to Amnesty International, there have been several cases of tuberculosis, but almost no access to medical treatment. Prisoners' uniforms are little more than

In some US prisons, death row inmates spend up to 20–23 hours alone in their cells. They leave their cells to shower (often handcuffed) and to exercise in a restricted area often called a 'recreation cage'.

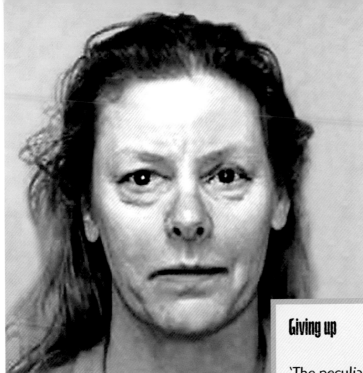

Aileen Wuornos spent over ten years on death row in Florida, USA, before being executed in 2002. Many women's prisons do not have 'death rows', and women are held in areas known as 'the hole'.

rags. Similarly overcrowded and unhygienic conditions also exist in several Caribbean countries.

What are conditions like in the USA?

Death-row prisoners in the USA do not have to face such hardships. However, condemned prisoners are held in a separate area from other prisoners, and, in many cases, have fewer rights to exercise, education and socialising time. One exception to this is Missouri, where prisoners under death sentence form part of the prison's general population, and have access to the same facilities.

Until the mid-1980s, most death-row prisoners in the USA were confined in their cells for long periods, and given very little opportunity for socialising or exercise. Various court cases have publicised these conditions, and states have instituted reforms to humanise death-row conditions. For example, in Texas, inmates regarded as capable of work are given jobs and given the privileges of ordinary prisoners, though

Giving up

'The peculiar silence of death row stems from the empty and ultimately lifeless regime imposed on the condemned. These offenders, seen as unfit to live in even the prison community, are relegated to this prison within a prison... Worn down in small and almost imperceptible ways, they gradually become less than fully human. At the end, they give in, they give up, and submit: yielding themselves to the execution team and the machinery of death.'

Source: *Death Work*, Robert Johnson

they are still separated from them. Those incapable of work (for mental, physical or security reasons) are granted at least 15 hours a week out-of-cell recreation time. This might include opportunities to exercise, dine with other death row prisoners and attend religious services.

What Is The Future Of Capital Punishment?

During the second half of the 20th century, there was a worldwide trend towards the abolition of capital punishment. The question remains as to whether this trend will continue and result in the global abolition of the practice. Out of 195 countries, there are still 83 that retain the death penalty.

The Turkish parliament, which abolished the death penalty in August 2002.

Life for a life

'We oppose the death penalty not just for what it does to those guilty of heinous crimes, but for what it does to all of us: it offers the tragic illusion that we can defend life by taking life.'

Most Reverend Joseph A Fiorenza, President, National Conference of Catholic Bishops, 1999

IN A FEW COUNTRIES there has even been an extension of the death penalty to cover new crimes, such as currency speculation (buying and selling for profit) and terrorism. More than 30 countries have made drug trafficking a capital offence, and in Singapore, the death penalty is imposed for possessing even a small amount of illegal drugs. There are, however, signs that the use of the death penalty is actually in decline. Many of the countries that officially

Governor Robert Ehrlich of Maryland, who lifted the suspension on executions in the state in January 2003, eight months after the suspension was imposed.

retain the death penalty actually employ this method of punishment quite rarely. In most years, only about 30 countries carry out executions. Four-fifths of these take place in just three countries – China, Iran and the USA.

In the USA, a large proportion – nearly three-quarters – of all executions since 1976 have occurred in just six states. In other words, a change of policy in just a few countries and states would drastically reduce the numbers of people executed around the world.

Other countries and states have gone so far as to suspend the use of the death penalty in recent years. Guatemala, Kyrgyzstan, the Philippines and the US state of Maryland all announced moratoria (suspensions) of the death penalty in 2002 and 2003. This may well be the start of a trend – allowing countries to end the use of capital punishment while still leaving themselves the option to reinstate it in future should they decide to.

Capital punishment is a problematic issue because it involves many moral as well as practical questions. Do governments have the right to put people to death? Does the death penalty actually make society safer by removing the criminal completely? Are there other forms of punishment that are fairer both to the accused and the victim? There are no clear-cut answers to these questions, and the debate looks set to continue for many years to come.

REFERENCE

COUNTRIES THAT HAVE ABOLISHED THE DEATH PENALTY FOR ALL CRIMES

Country	Date of abolition for ordinary crimes	Date of abolition	Date of last execution
Andorra		1990	1943
Angola		1992	
Australia	1984	1985	1967
Austria	1950	1968	1950
Azerbaijan		1998	1993
Belgium		1996	1950
Bulgaria		1998	1989
Cambodia		1989	
Canada	1976	1998	1962
Cape Verde		1981	1835
Colombia		1910	1909
Costa Rica		1877	
Côte d'Ivoire		2000	
Croatia		1990	
Cyprus	1983	2002	1962
Czech Republic		1990	
Denmark	1933	1978	1950
Dominican Republic		1966	
East Timor		1999	
Ecuador		1906	
Estonia		1998	1991
Finland	1949	1972	1944
France		1981	1977
Georgia		1997	1994*
Germany		1987	
Guinea-Bissau		1993	1986*
Haiti		1987	1972*
Honduras		1956	1940
Hungary		1990	1988
Iceland		1928	1830
Ireland		1990	1954
Italy	1947	1994	1947
Liechtenstein		1987	1785
Lithuania		1998	1995
Luxembourg		1979	1949
Macedonia		1991	
Malta	1971	2000	1943
Mauritius		1995	1987

Country	Date of abolition for ordinary crimes	Date of abolition	Date of last execution
Moldova		1995	
Monaco		1962	1847
Mozambique		1990	1986
Namibia		1990	1988*
Nepal	1990	1997	1979
Netherlands	1870	1982	1952
New Zealand	1961	1989	1957
Nicaragua		1979	1930
Norway	1905	1997	1948
Paraguay		1992	1928
Poland		1997	1988
Portugal	1867	1976	1849*
Romania		1989	1989
San Marino	1848	1865	1468*
Slovak Republic		1990	
Slovenia		1989	
South Africa	1995	1997	1991
Spain	1978	1995	1975
Sweden	1921	1972	1910
Switzerland	1942	1992	1944
Turkmenistan		1999	
Ukraine		1999	
UK	1973	1998	1964
Uruguay		1907	
Vatican City State		1969	
Venezuela		1863	
Yugoslavia		2002	

*= date of last known execution

'Ordinary crimes' includes crimes such as murder, but does not include exceptional crimes such as military offences or crimes against humanity.

Columns with no entry indicate that information is unavailable for that country.

COUNTRIES THAT HAVE ABOLISHED THE DEATH PENALTY FOR ALL BUT EXCEPTIONAL CRIMES, SUCH AS MILITARY OFFENCES OR CRIMES AGAINST HUMANITY

Country	Date of abolition for ordinary crimes	Date of last execution
Albania	2000	1995
Argentina	1984	1916
Bolivia	1997	1974
Brazil	1979	1855
Chile	2001	1991
El Salvador	1983	1973*
Fiji	1979	1964
Greece	1993	1972
Israel	1954	1962
Latvia	1999	1996
Peru	1979	1979
Turkey	2002	1984

*= date of last known execution

COUNTRIES THAT OFFICIALLY RETAIN THE DEATH PENALTY FOR ORDINARY CRIMES, SUCH AS MURDER, BUT HAVE NOT EXECUTED ANYONE SINCE 1990 OR HAVE MADE AN INTERNATIONAL COMMITMENT NOT TO USE THE DEATH PENALTY

Country	Date of last execution
Bhutan	1964*
Brunei Darussalam	1957*
Burkina Faso	1988
Central African Republic	1981
Congo (Republic)	1982
Gambia	1981
Grenada	1978
Madagascar	1958*
Maldives	1952*
Mali	1980
Niger	1976*
Papua New Guinea	1950
Russian Federation	1996*
Senegal	1967
Sri Lanka	1976
Suriname	1982
Tonga	1982

*= date of last known execution

COUNTRIES THAT RETAIN THE DEATH PENALTY

Afghanistan, Algeria, Antigua and Barbuda, Armenia , Bahamas, Bahrain, Bangladesh, Barbados, Belarus, Belize, Benin, Botswana, Burundi, Cameroon, Chad, China, Comoros, Congo (Democratic Republic), Cuba, Dominica, Egypt, Equatorial Guinea, Eritrea, Ethiopia, Gabon, Ghana, Guatemala, Guinea, Guyana, India, Indonesia, Iran, Iraq, Jamaica, Japan, Jordan, Kazakhstan, Kenya, Kuwait, Kyrgyzstan, Laos, Lebanon, Lesotho, Liberia, Libya, Malawi, Malaysia, Mauritania, Mongolia, Morocco, Myanmar, Nigeria, North Korea, Oman, Pakistan, Palestinian Authority, Philippines, Qatar, Rwanda, Saint Christopher and Nevis, Saint Lucia, Saint Vincent and Grenadines, Saudi Arabia, Sierra Leone, Singapore, Somalia, South Korea, Sudan, Swaziland, Syria, Taiwan, Tajikistan, Tanzania, Thailand, Trinidad and Tobago, Tunisia, Uganda, United Arab Emirates, United States of America, Uzbekistan, Vietnam, Yemen, Zambia and Zimbabwe

---

RECORDED EXECUTIONS OF CHILD OFFENDERS SINCE 1990: CASE DETAILS

Country	Name of prisoner	Age	Date of execution
Dem Rep of Congo	Kasongo	14 ate	15 January 2000
Iran	Ebrahim Qorbanzadeh	17 ate	24 October 1999
	Jasem Abrahimi	17 ate	14 January 2000
	Mehrdad Yousefi	16 ato	29 May 2001
Nigeria	Chiebore Onuoha	15 ato	31 July 1997
Pakistan	Shamun Masih	14 ato	30 September 1997
	Ali Sher	13 ato	3 November 2001
USA	Dalton Prejean	17 ato	18 May 1990
	Johnny Garrett	17 ato	11 February 1992
	Curtis Harris	17 ato	1 July 1993
	Frederick Lashley	17 ato	28 July 1993
	Christopher Burger	17 ato	7 December 1993
	Ruben Cantu	17 ato	24 August 1993
	Joseph John Cannon	17 ato	22 April 1998
	Robert Anthony Carter	17 ato	18 May 1998
	Sean Sellers	16 ato	4 February 1999
	Steve Roach	17 ato	10 January 2000
	Chris Thomas	17 ato	13 January 2000
	Glen McGinnis	17 ato	25 January 2000
	Gary Graham	17 ato	22 June 2000
	Gerald Mitchell	17 ato	22 October 2001
	Napolean Beazley	17 ato	28 May 2002
	TJ Jones	17 ato	8 August 2002
	Toronto Patterson	17 ato	28 August 2002
	Scott Allen Hain	17 ato	3 April 2003

ate = at time of execution
ato = at time of offence

Source for all statistics in this section: Amnesty International

GLOSSARY

adultery Sexual relations between a married person and someone other than his or her spouse.

apostasy The rejection by a person of a religious belief.

appeal The hearing of a previously tried case in a superior court, or a request for such a hearing.

arson The crime of deliberately setting something, such as a building, on fire.

attorney A qualified lawyer, who represents a defendant in court.

authoritarian A non-democratic style of government that requires obedience to a ruling person or group.

bereavement Loss of a loved one.

blasphemy Disrespect for sacred things.

clemency An act of forgiveness or mercy.

commute Reduce a legal sentence to a less severe one.

conviction Finding someone guilty of a crime.

crucifixion A form of execution used in ancient times in which a person is bound or nailed to an upright cross until they are dead.

death row An area in a prison housing prisoners who have been sentenced to be executed.

defendant A person accused of a crime and required to appear in court.

deterrent Something that discourages a person or a group from acting in a certain way.

DNA testing A method of identifying someone by analysing their DNA. DNA is a type of molecule found in every cell of every living thing. It carries genetic information which determines how we look and how we act.

electric chair A chair used to execute people who have been sentenced to death by passing an electric current through them.

embezzlement Taking for personal use the money that has been given on trust by others, without their knowledge or permission.

exempt Release someone from a rule that applies to others.

federal prisoners Prisoners who have been convicted of breaking federal law, as opposed to the law of a state, in the United States.

firing squad A group of soldiers who carry out an execution by gunfire.

homicide The unlawful killing of another human being.

Hudud An Arabic word used to describe crimes which have fixed punishments, laid down in the Qur'an. A judge has no power to override such punishments, and no pardon is possible.

interrogator Someone who questions somebody thoroughly, often in an aggressive or threatening manner.

judge A high-ranking court officer who supervises trials, instructs juries and pronounces sentence.

jurisdiction The power to make legal judgments, or the area over which legal authority extends.

jury A group of people, usually numbering 12, chosen to give a verdict on a legal case that is presented to them in a court of law.

juvenile A young person.

legislature An official body, usually chosen by election, with the power to make, change and repeal laws.

lethal injection A form of execution in which a prisoner is injected with poisonous drugs in order to cause his or her death.

life imprisonment A punishment in which someone who has been convicted of a crime must spend the rest of his or her life in prison.

miscarriage of justice A failure of a country's legal system to come to a fair or correct decision.

moratorium A formally agreed period during which a particular activity, such as capital punishment, is halted.

parole The early release of a prisoner, with conditions such as good behaviour and regular reporting to the authorities for a stated period of time.

prosecution The trial of somebody in a court of law for a criminal offence.

public defender An attorney who represents defendants who cannot afford their own lawyer.

ratify Give formal approval of something, usually an agreement negotiated by someone else, so that it becomes valid and operative.

resolution A formal agreement arrived at during a meeting, and usually as a result of a vote.

sabotage Causing the deliberate damaging or destruction of property or equipment.

Shari'ah Islamic religious law.

signatory A person, organisation or government that has signed a treaty and is bound by it.

terrorism The use of violence against civilians and political leaders in order to achieve political aims.

treason The crime of betraying one's own country.

United Nations An organisation of countries, formed in 1945, to promote peace, security and international cooperation around the world. Its headquarters are in New York City.

vengeance Punishment inflicted in return for a wrong.

verdict The finding of a jury on a case presented to it in a trial.

wean Start feeding a baby food other than its mother's milk.

FURTHER INFORMATION

BOOKS

Death and Justice, Mark Fuhrman, William Morrow & Co 2003

Capital Punishment: Issues and Perspectives, AV Mandel, Nova Science Publishing 2003

The Leviathan's Choice: Capital Punishment in the Twenty-first Century, J Michael Martinez, William D Richardson, D Brandon Hornsby, Rowman & Littlefield Publishers 2003

The Death Penalty: A Worldwide Perspective, Roger Hood, Oxford University Press 2002

Just the Facts: Capital Punishment, [author not known], Heinemann 2004

Open for Debate: Capital Punishment, Ron Fridell, Marshall Cavendish 2003

Point/Counterpoint Books: Capital Punishment, Alan Marzilli (editor), Chelsea House 2003

At Issue: Is the Death Penalty Fair?, Mary E Williams, Greenhaven Press 2003

WEBSITES

http://www.religioustolerance.org/execute.htm
Information on capital punishment, and arguments for and against, including religious perspectives on the issue.

http://www.helsinki.fi/~tuschano/cp
Provides links to websites on the history of capital punishment – organised by country.

http://www.utm.edu/research/iep/c/capitalp.htm
Arguments for and against capital punishment, from the Internet Encyclopaedia of Philosophy.

http://www.deathpenaltyinfo.org/index.php
The Death Penalty Information Center is against capital punishment. Its website provides information and statistics about the death penalty, mainly in the USA.

http://web.amnesty.org/pages/deathpenalty_index_eng?openview
Amnesty International campaigns against the death penalty. Its website is packed with up-to-date facts and figures about the death penalty worldwide.

http://www.prodeathpenalty.com
This website is in favour of capital punishment, and presents arguments and statistics that support its views.

ORGANISATIONS

Opposed to the death penalty, or in favour of death penalty reform:

American Civil Liberties Union
125 Broad Street, 18th Floor,
New York, NY 10004
USA
Tel: +1 212 549 2585
Website:
http://www.aclu.org/safeandfree

Amnesty International
99–119 Rosebery Avenue,
London, EC1R 4RE, UK
Tel: 020 7814 6200
Website: http://www.amnesty.org.uk

ABA Death Penalty Representation Project
727 15th Street, NW, 9th Floor,
Washington, DC 20005
USA
Tel: +1 202 662 1738
Fax: +1 202 662 8649
Website:
http://www.abanet.org/deathpenalty

Citizens United for Alternatives to the Death Penalty
PMB 297, 177 US Highway #1,
Tequesta, FL 33469
USA
Tel: +1 800 973 6548
Website: http://www.cuadp.org

Death Penalty Information Center
1320 18th Street NW, 5th Floor,
Washington, DC 20036
USA
Tel: +1 202 293 6970
Fax: +1 202 822 4787
Website:
http://www.deathpenaltyinfo.org

Prison Activist Resource Center (PARC)
PO Box 339, Berkeley CA 94701
USA
Tel: +1 510 893 4648
Fax: +1 510 893 4607
Website: http://www.prisonactivists.org

Murder Victims Families for Reconciliation
2161 Massachusetts Avenue,
Cambridge, MA 02140
USA
Tel: +1 617 868 0007
Fax: +1 617 354 2832
Website: http://www.mvfr.org

The National Coalition to Abolish the Death Penalty
920 Pennsylvania Ave. SE,
Washington, DC 20003
USA
Tel: +1 202 543 9577
Fax: +1 202 543 7798
Website: http://www.ncadp.org

In favour of the death penalty:

Justice For All
Aramco Building Auditorium
9009 W 610 Loop at N Braeswood,
Houston, Texas
USA
Tel: +1 713 935 9300

National Center for Policy Analysis
12655 N Central Expressway, Suite 720,
Dallas, Texas
USA
Tel: +1 972 386 6272
Fax: +1 972 386 0924

INDEX